WHAT TURNS UP

What Turns Up

Michael Glover

What Turns Up

Copyright © Michael Glover 2022

All rights reserved. The moral rights of the author have been asserted.

Cover © 1889 books

www.1889books

ISBN: 978-1-915045-10-2

Other publications by Michael Glover

Poetry:

Measured Lives (1994)
Impossible Horizons (1995)
A Small Modicum of Folly (1997)
The Bead-Eyed Man (1999)
Amidst All This Debris (2001)
For the Sheer Hell of Living (2008)
Only So Much (2011)
Hypothetical May Morning (2018)
Messages to Federico (2018)
What You Do With Days (2019)
One Season in Hell (2020)
The Timely Lift-Off of the Famous Harlequin-Fish (2022)

Others:

Headlong into Pennilessness (2011)
Great Works: Encounters with Art (2016)
Playing Out in the Wireless Days (2017)
111 Places in Sheffield You Should Not Miss (2017)
Late Days (2018)
Neo Rauch (2019)
The Book of Extremities (2019)
Thrust (2019)
John Ruskin: an idiosyncratic dictionary (2019)
Rose Wylie (2020)
The Trapper (2021)
Nellie's Devils (2022)

As editor or contributor:

Memories of Duveen Brothers (1976)
Goin' down, down, down: Matthew Ronay (2006)
Between Eagles and Pioneers: Georg Baselitz (2011)
Robert Therrien (2016)
Monique Frydman (2017)

*For my Sheffield pals
Mick and Kay*

Contents

Foreword	1
Just the Three of Us	2
Shined Shoes	3
Your Star	4
Hardy Daisies	5
Rose	6
Past Her	7
Mayday	8
Not Taking No for an Answer	9
Rough Stuff	10
Really Feeling It	11
Pulling Yourself Together	12
Saturday Night	13
Losing It	14
Blocking the Door	15
The Allotment	16
General Malarkey	17
John	18
Back There Then	19
Back There Then	20
Riotous Assembly	21
Poem	22
Being Lit Up	23
Having a House	24
Losing	25
The Poster	26
Sandpaper	27
Something of the Sort	28
The Interruption	29
How Things Are	30
Catching Up	31
Nowhere in Particular	32
Asking about Windows	33
Doreen	34
Props	35

Never Enough	36
Shut Door	37
Two Christmases	38
Saying Yes or No	39
Perfect Fit	40
Puzzling Times	41
Chats	42
Coins	43
Where?	44
Off to the Shop	45
Philosopher	46
Different Habits	47
Scrattin	48
The Thinnest Slivver	49
The Paper	50
The Dandelion Clock	51
All There Is to Be Said	52

Foreword

What prompts any book into being? It's a bit of a mystery, always will be, which is a good thing, of course. Who wants to know what he's going to write before he writes it? That would be no fun. This one started off as a headlong flight from frustration. I had been struggling to write a rather pretentious piece of extended prose set in Paris (where else?), with Samuel Beckett and various French writers at my back, all smoking together in a small room, egging me on. Sartre was just about to arrive. It was twelve thousand words in and rapidly going nowhere.

Then someone sent me a book of poems[1] through the post with a picture of a young couple on the cover standing outside a house. He was holding a baby as if it might just be a bit of a burden. His hair was tousled as if he wasn't long out of bed. She looked a bit surly in her panda-toed house slippers. Were they happy?

It was a snap of an any-sort-of-a-day situation, and yet I felt very moved by its sheer ordinariness. I wrote a little poem about it. Then poems in a similar mood started to write themselves, day after day, straight out, unembellished, unassuming, no frills, no thoughts of metaphors or similes, no dreams of literary achievement, simple – yet perhaps not so simple in their feelings after all. I think of them as having emerged from Sheffeld, my home town, but they were not written in Sheffeldish because this time I didn't want some idiot to regard my words as a jokey caricature of proper human speech. Whatever that may be.

---

1 https://www.bloodaxebooks.com/ecs/product/where-now-begins-1240

Just the Three of Us

The three of us posed for the snap
in front of the gate.
I carried the nipper in my arms.
Your lick of blond hair fell forward
onto your forehead.
You looked none too happy
for all you were wearing
those panda house slippers...

Happiness? Nothing guarantees it.
Years later I think back to it,
and how my hair looked tousled.
There's promise in tousled hair,
and a bit of a come-on too –
if only I'd known it.

Shined Shoes

Life is long in the stirring.
You add a bit of spice now and again –
a tease of a girl in a skirt,
hurrying away, then gone altogether.

Life comes and goes as it chooses.
So much of it all at once,
and then so little.
Was it catching up you were always so bad at?

Life flickers like an old film.
You can barely see it at all some days.
Then it gets clear all over again.
Shined shoes in the sunshine.

I never asked for too much.
Life was a bit of a waiting game.
You lose something, you win back the same old rubbish.
I wouldn't say no if it were all on offer.

Your Star

There's no going back to any of that.
The house has gone, and you with it.
What was the last thing you said to me?
That I couldn't balance a pea on my hat
   to save my life?
Let's call that ridiculous just for the sake of it.

We've both gone our ways, differently.
I discuss rawl plugs in this shop
with customers blown this way for a bit of chat.
Nothing comes easy.
You scrub floors, you tell me,
when the old folks let you.

I only remember my favourite bits –
a particular colour of a party frock,
and how you flounced around when you wore it.
You were always the star of our show,
and my applause always genuine enough
until it faltered and stopped.

Hardy Daisies

The flower lady came by
with a fat bunch of daisies in her fist.
Feeling pity, you gave her a mite,
at which she seemed pleased as does Punch
when he smacks down his Judy.

We put the daisies in the window.
They go on and on if you let them.
Flowers that cost lots die on you –
not so daisies.
They stay there, looking out,
pleased as punch to be common.
Just like the two of us, my lady.

Rose

I never said to you then
what I'm going to say now,
not in so many words anyway.
In fact, in no words at all
because words never came easy.

It was your hands that were always so lovely,
and how you folded them over
as if they were a perfect ft for each other.
I never held them. I never touched them.

You may still be listening. Just.

Past Her

I want nothing of you
but what I already have, she said,
glancing back at his shadow
which sloped so tenderly down the doorframe.

Think nothing of it, he replied,
the sun bright in his eyes
to such an extent that
he had to look past her.

And still he goes on looking,
day in, day out, and forever after,
past her and past her and past her.

Mayday

It's only that other Mayday I remember.
(You weren't there though, were you?)
The grass was damp, the pop in the bottle too watery.
The band came along, and I smiled them all down,
being a child, with both legs drumming like crazy.

It was Mayday, always Mayday on that day,
and the rain was teeming.
Macs on! Hurry! Hysterical giggles.
Back home, we slipped out of Mayday in a jiffy.

I loved it, Mayday.
The thought of it still thrills me,
and all that I was back then,
a child top-to-toe for sure,
all daft and skittery.

Not Taking No for an Answer

You walked straight past, barely noticeable,
on your way to the bus stop,
carrying a haversack on your back,
a smallish man made bigger
by the clothes you were wearing,
it being grey and thundery.

Next time, on the upper deck of the bus,
you were smoking with those finicky fingers.
Did you smile? I don't really remember.
When we did get together,
it lasted for years and years,
not all of them happy.

Some were though –
out in the garden,
heaving side by side
on a holly bush root
that just wouldn't take
no for an answer.

Rough Stuff

Was there much love-talk?
Or any other talk really?
You weren't much for words, were you?

We did like walking though,
side by side, hip to hip,
on a sunny day,
or picking our way
across the stepping stones
in the Rivelin Valley,
with the brook rushing under,
inviting a slippage then fall
that never quite happened.

We'd pause, flush-faced,
by the bank,
and chew on a sandwich,
then lie back side by side,
letting everything settle
under a drift of blue sky,
all that rough stuff
that came between us.

Really Feeling It

You left when you did.
That's all there was to it, really.
It came down to paperwork in the end.
You were quite nice to me,
about the arrangements.

I kept him happy.
I saw to his needs.
I loved him. And he loved me.
You didn't get much
of a look-in, did you?

Not that you'd asked to.
Not that you'd really wanted.
He wanted you though,
in the night was when he said it,
calling out in the dark.
That's when we really felt it.

Pulling Yourself Together

Did we ever pose for a photo?
I mean a serious one,
not one at the seaside, being silly?
Not that I recall.
We never dressed up –
suit, dress, hat –
nothing like that.

Perhaps we were
altogether too sloppy
in our habits,
perhaps if we'd
pulled ourselves together,
as mum used to say,
we'd have made something
out of all of our days together.

Saturday Night

It being a Saturday night,
the lads are out in force,
playing a blinder
without a ball.

What big voices they've got!
The rude songs never stop
because no one wants
to stop laughing...

They'll regret it later,
staring down into a tea mug,
being watched over
by mum with a plastic bowl,
and a thunderous look down
at the state of the carpet.

Losing It

There's so much to be said
for every day that comes along.
It even happened here every once in a while –
that look that you gave me,
the way the breeze mussed up your hair,
a joke or two shared.
Nothing much else was needed.

It's funny to think I didn't know you
before I knew you,
that you'd been a stranger once,
just another, any other, man.
Then we lost it all again
just as if it had never been.

How did that happen?
Who made it all drain away,
day after day?
Who neglected what and why?
Why did all the talk dry up
and our hands never want to touch?

Blocking the Door

Don't you try and soft-soap me, feller.
I've got my head screwed on right, let me tell you.
I saw you for what you were
the moment you blocked the door
with your cock-sure, hale-and-hearty manner
and all that big talk of days at the Doncaster Races.

Flowers won't cut it with me neither,
not when you pick off the label.
Cut-price, full-price, what have you,
you're a con artist in a trilby,
and that's pretty well all there is to it, matey.

The Allotment
for Mick

Down at the allotment Crosspool way,
the big feller was wrenching out daisies
until he went red in the face.

I was choosing rhubarb sticks by the hedge,
fat ones and thin,
lopping them off with a knife
blunt enough to cut butter.

One or two potatoes were peeking out,
as if to say: just you dare...
I did dare!
Two dozen or more!

Alan was sizing up his shed,
pride of his life since his girl left him.
He sobbed once over her
next to the water butt.

That would have been last summer.

General Malarkey

Sometimes it's you that turns up,
half sozzled or not,
hovering by the door,
rolled programme in hand,
to discuss Saturday's match.
Again. I let you in.

Sometimes it's you that says:
Let's go out then!
We've stayed in enough!
Have we? Have we? I say back,
pointing at the rain.
There's always more tea in the pot.

Sometimes I'm thinking to myself:
not him again! I just can't bear it.
And then, seconds later, you're back,
and we're stuck into a nice chat
about all the malarkey that's going off.

John

You just took yourself off,
leaving a gap in the world.
What did you do it for?
Who asked you?
What darkness descended?

Perhaps I never knew you
when I knew you.
Perhaps that smile
wasn't a smile after all.

Perhaps you were looking
right past me
to the blank space
where no one else
could ever be with you.

Back There Then

If I took you back there,
showed you the spot,
what would you think?
Would you be happy?

It was where it happened,
like it or not,
when I saw you and you saw me.
Whenever that was.

It hasn't changed a lot.
A bit more rubbish in the hedge.
Pub knocked down.
A bench to sit on

if we should ever want to.

Back There Then

I always walked in a straight line.
Not like you, all over the place.
Was it that that made us two of a kind?
I doubt it.

Riotous Assembly

Life just happens.
You have to face it.
Nobody asked for it.
Nobody can walk away.

Standing together helps,
even in old clothes,
even when you're half deaf,
even when you haven't a clue what's going off.

Poem

Anybody could have written that!
Trouble is I just did.
Don't you try getting in on the act,
with your big mouth and your daft gesturings.

Being Lit Up

When the lights came back on,
you were still carrying the sandwiches.
The streets were as busy as ever.
Nobody had left. Nobody had bellowed.

When the lights came back on,
I was squeezing your hand on the sofa.
Somebody said Christmas for a lark,
then left the door open to freezing air.

When the lights came back on,
I wasn't as young as I had been.
Still, I can think of many reasons to complain,
and being lit up isn't one of them.

Having a House

All we ever needed was a house.
Rattling around just didn't suit.
To be stuck inside four walls
would keep everything together just nicely.

So you bought me a house,
and I chipped in with the trimmings:
wide-screen, fat leather sofa, two books,
everything you ever fill a house with.

When the walls fell down all at once,
we were lucky, being in the garden.
We stared back at it all: nice as pie,
everything as it had been – barring skimmings of dust.

Losing

There's a lot still to lose,
and a lot lost already.
I haven't counted it all up.
I've been far too busy

in the sunlight, making hay,
in the moonlight, crooning like a wolf,
in the daytime, cashing in on all the good luck
someone once vaguely promised me.

There's a lot still to lose,
and I lot I could lose for you,
with these quicksilver hands,
and a certain way with the promises.

The Poster

Do you happen to know
how long you'll be standing there,
staring at that poster?

And whether, when I approach,
you'll say a word or two about it,
as if we knew each other already?

That would certainly be my wish.
As for you, who's to guess?
You haven't even seen me yet.

Sandpaper

He reminded me of sandpaper,
so rough and so ready was he.
The smile was invented
the day after they buried him.

Something of the Sort

If you could only talk,
I'd be prepared to listen.
It's not that much to ask.
No money changes hands.

If you could say yes or no,
I'd know whether we were going.
As it is, I sit here on this chair
to the tune of nothing happening.

Did love ever come up?
Something of the sort.
We've held hands once or twice,
your cold ones inside mine.

The Interruption

This is what I was saying before you interrupted me.
You understand now why I had to say it,
and how much it would have meant to me.
I'm pleased to get shot of it at last.
I'm pleased to soften the pain
of giving birth to such words as these
because it's all about honesty, honesty, honesty.

It's taken me a long time to come clean,
even to know how to say what I had to say.
It's both simple and complicated.
It's like trying to undo the tightest of knots
in a very thin piece of string,
if you get my meaning,
if you understand my drift.

I went at it for days in my head
even before I wrote anything down.
Yes, I wrote it all down in the end
because that was the only way to
make sure that I was being truthful
and thoroughgoing and even brutal with myself.
And now you won't even let me finish, will you?

How Things Are

If you were to say *this is the last of it*,
you'd be bang on target
because it's all I want too.

I never wanted things to drag on.
I wanted it, always, to be short, sharp and funny.
And that's what it was, and now isn't, often.

So listen to this:

I understand when a door slams,
I understand about last words ever,
I understand about night following day.

Things have always been like this.

Catching Up

I caught up with you
half way through.
You hadn't changed that much.
Perhaps not quite so fast
as in the past.

The look was the same,
that same stealthy turning away,
giving me the shoulder.
I quite liked that now
because it's all so familiar.

Like a tune I play and re-play
on an old record player
with a blunt copper needle,
so many crackles and jumps,
and then

clunk and repeat,
clunk and repeat,
clunk and repeat,
until you feel like
chucking it through the bloody window.

Nowhere in Particular

Every now and again, your eyes glaze,
and you turn away and window-gaze
and start thinking about something else.

Hello, love, I say,
smacking your knee ever so gently.
A faint smile comes back
as you turn to face me.

What is it? you say.
Where were you? I say back.
Oh nowhere, you say.
Any particular nowhere? I ask.

No, just any old nowhere that comes along.

Asking about Windows

What are windows for?
To sit on the other side of,
in silence,
staring out at all the noise.

What are windows for?
To see yourself in now and again
when you least expected it,
sometimes younger,
sometimes older on a bad day.

What are windows for?
To lean against
like an angel or a ghost
suspended from nothing at all.

What are windows for?
Stop asking daft questions
when the answer's so obvious, thicko.

Doreen

The light came on,
the one you'd just switched off.
No amount of fiddling with the switch
or the fuse box
made it change its mind.
God's up to something, you said.
Brace yourself for a calamity, Doreen.

Props

You never used many words.
You weren't that sort of a chap.
And the ones you did use
were picked up from elsewhere,
odd phrases to try to make me laugh.

It wasn't all bad.
You were good with the little jobs.
And I made up for it
by finding words in library books
that you sometimes used
to prop up a table leg
when you needed an even surface.

Never Enough

I'm not planning to go back any time soon.
There was nothing to see anyway.
And the weather was always rubbish.
Why did you choose it in the first place?

You know I hate pokey flats,
even when you get a view of the sea.
But when you can't see the sea for mist,
and every day you're never wearing enough...

You said that was the beginning of the end.
It wasn't meant to be like that.
Holidays are for having the best times of your life.
Holidays are for blowing loads of money you haven't got.

Shut Door

Why are they all standing over there?
Do they know something we don't know?
It's a perfectly ordinary house
with a door shut fast.

Why don't you ask them if you really want to know?
Because, unlike you, I'm not a nosey parker
        through and through.
I'm just a curious person, always have been,
and you generally don't see that sort of thing.

Usually if there's loads of people gathered,
there's talk and lots of commotion,
and if you're outside a door like that one for long,
somebody opens it and says something sensible.

Two Christmases

Last Christmas you were all smiles and giggles
       and red cheeks.
This time around you don't even want to know me.
I'm still around, you know. I haven't gone anywhere.

I watched you going to the bin with the wrapping paper
in that grey cardigan, pulled tight against the weather.
You didn't even look up. You must have seen me.

I wasn't going to be the first one to speak.
After all, I was the one with the grievance
big as a fat wodge of your mother's pastry.

Saying Yes or No

I didn't hear you say no.
I thought you'd say yes.
Otherwise, I wouldn't have come at all.
I wouldn't have wasted my breath.

I'm not used to being treated badly.
Girls usually take a shine to me.
The clothes are good, teeth too.
I've got a pocketful of money.

So what is it then?
What happened to stop it?
It's no good saying it never started.
You were the one that looked at me.

Perfect Fit

If I said I'd go back any day now,
I meant it.
Unlike you, stuffed full of holy boloney.
No one could have invented you.

Where did you get that hat?
You surely didn't buy it.
God dropped it on your head,
and then said: perfect fit, angel.

I don't know why I bother.
I don't know why I wait for you.
Hymns just go on and on, don't they?
I've brought the dog along with me.

Puzzling Times

It's a testing time for all of us,
having you asleep in that corner
with no knowing when
you might wake up.

No one knows how it happened.
No one knows when it will end.
It doesn't seem right putting the tea things out
without your constant jabber.

I look down at you a lot.
I sit on a chair and tell you things –
who's going past the window in a huff,
how much the washing's building up.

Luckily Pat comes every day,
matter of fact as ever,
telling me to cheer up for goodness sake.
There's not any really bad news yet, she says.

Chats

I thought I'd get the good news in first.
There's rain forecast for every day barring one.
Which means we can have nice little chats
on the phone to cheer ourselves up.

The one thing to be said just now is this:
I need a new pair of shoes in the usual size.
I've been putting it off since September.
They just about got me through last summer.

You weren't very well the last time we went out.
I wouldn't overdo it if I were you.
Once a week would be enough for me.
You can always send me those shoes for Christmas.

Coins

I've always kept coins in a jar,
old coins, new coins, odd as they come.
Some of them are still good for spending.
Some of them are rare enough to be worth something.

I like pouring them out, sorting them through,
by shape, size, look, general feel.
The one with the emperor's so smooth and faded,
you can't really tell if it's man or potato.

I keep a few of them in my trouser pockets,
the ones I can spend when I feel like it.
Shaking coins up and down, letting them slip through
        the fingers,
makes you feel you might just get up to a bit of mischief.

Where?

Where do we go from here?
Words aren't up to much.
We just make more mess when we use them,
like little kids slopping paint.

I don't know why I'm writing this down at all.
I've already told you I've given up,
that I've got no breath left for talking,
that it's all a blank now, a blundering forward.

So we should both shut up.
And, no, Fred,
I don't think a daft smile would do
just as well instead.

Off to the Shop

Some nights we just lay there staring up,
breathing, not even thinking.
You had a lovely warmth about you, never hot,
and never fidgety. You were always so serene.

I liked that, being your opposite, I mean.
I could never stay still for a second,
talking, always, twenty to the dozen.
You said so little, and the words were always so well chosen.

I never really knew why you took yourself off.
You said you liked it, our differences, I mean.
You never talked about it. You never came clean.
You just had to leave, and then not in a hurry.

Just off to the shop read what you wrote, so neatly.

Philosopher

When you start thinking about
all that there is to be thought about,
you feel weary enough to go back to bed –
bills, bad weather tomorrow, the next shop...

Who in their right mind would stand for it?
There's no other way though, is there, love?
I can't expect you to fix all that
on top of everything else that turns up.

You always tell me you do too much already,
and I do too little, that you're sick
of me talking so much tosh
when I spend half the day in bed, smoking.

Different Habits

A bit later on he stopped off for a chat.
I let it happen – like everything else.
He's nice enough, I suppose.
I don't begrudge him being who he was.

It's when it's too often that it gets my goat.
Privacy's what I like most of all,
being alone with the television on,
half dozing, nursing a nice cup of tea.

That's not your idea of a life?
Everyone's different. Live and let be.
Some folks are forever nosey-parkering.
Others keep themselves to themselves.

Scrattin

She never stayed still for a single moment,
forever had to be at it, at it,
dubbinnin the doorstep, shining the hob,
plinky-plonking the duster down the upright piano.

Then off to the shops, just before closing,
catching at the tail end of a bargain –
veg on the turn, fish fingers left out in the sun,
yesterday's daily paper free for the asking.

Scrattin. Scrattin. Scrattin. Scrattin,
thin as a pipe cleaner from all that bustle,
things to be done, plant pots washed spotless
of all that mucky earth under a favourite blossom.

The Thinnest Slivver

He came out with it at suppertime.
I'd just put out the cheddar and the crackers.
He blew on my neck – he always did that,
but when I turned, he wasn't smiling.

He said there was no good time to say it.
He said he'd meant to tell me before.
He said he didn't want to hurt me,
but he knew there was no alternative.

I kept on arranging his fork and his knife.
It was all I could think to do just then.
Then I sliced off the thinnest sliver of cheese,
and imagined how strong it tastes in your mouth.

The Paper

Going out to buy a paper,
that was the daily routine.
Scandalised by headlines.
Scanning the football results.

Spreading it over his face when the sun came out.
Twisting it into little spills to make the fire blaze up.
Making paper aeroplanes for a little kid.
Dumping it in the bin with all the rest.

Going out to buy it,
that's what got him up.
What else to get up for
on a day like any other?

And when he stopped buying it,
it meant that *he'd* stopped.
He just wasn't there any more
to bother with it.

The Dandelion Clock

You can blow a dandelion clock
until it's nothing at all –
just a damp tube inclined to bend
with a bald knob on top.

That's what life's like, I reckon,
what all it comes down to in the end.
I'm not asking you to agree with me,
my cussed old friend.

All there is to be said

This is about all there is to be said.
I think we gave it as good as we got.
No blame attached to either, of course.
Nothing could have been done otherwise.

You born over there, me in this street.
A passing chance pushing us together.
Lots of soft talk over beer, shandy, crisps.
That come-on way you looked at me.

Could it have lasted if we'd tried?
Only if we'd been different types.
We're fly-by-nights, the both of us,
here one minute, gone the next.

www.ingramcontent.com/pod-product-compliance
Lightning Source LLC
Chambersburg PA
CBHW030046100526
44590CB00011B/338